Coastal

For Sally
and Randy
with our
Love and
admiration

Betsy
and
Larry

Jane Duran

Coastal

ENITHARMON PRESS

First published in 2005
by Enitharmon Press
26B Caversham Road
London NW5 2DU

www.enitharmon.co.uk

Distributed in the UK by
Central Books
99 Wallis Road
London E9 5LN

Distributed in the USA and Canada
by Dufour Editions Inc.
PO Box 7, Chester Springs
PA 19425, USA

ISBN 1 900564 24 6

British Library Cataloguing-in-Publication Data.
A catalogue record for this book is available
from the British Library.

Typeset in Bembo by Servis Filmsetting Ltd
and printed in England by
Antony Rowe Ltd

for my mother
Bonté Romilly Duran
in memory

ACKNOWLEDGEMENTS

Some of these poems, or versions of these poems, first appeared in *Colorado Review, Poetry London, Poetry Review*; and in *New Writing 6* (Vintage in association with The British Council, 1997), *The New Exeter Book of Riddles* (Enitharmon Press, 1999) and *thetall-lighthouse Poetry Review* (2004).

My warm thanks to those who read and commented on versions of this manuscript or on the sequence *Zagharit*: Wendy Brandmark, Cheli Durán, Mimi Khalvati, Vivien Lewis, Sue MacIntyre, Sharon Morris, Syra Sowe, Bachir Taouti, Mary Williamson and Susan Wicks. I am very grateful to my editor Stephen Stuart-Smith for his constant support. My thanks above all to my husband Redha, my nephew Mounir Nini, and finally to my Thursday Group who are always an inspiration.

CONTENTS

Coastal

Coastal	*10*
Dementia	*12*
Cape Porpoise, Maine	*13*
Stroke	*14*
Overlays	*15*
Fish-houses	*19*
Coat	*20*
Hairpins	*21*
Whippoorwill	*22*
Blueberry Picking	*23*
Elvis	*24*
In the Paintings of Edward Hopper	*26*
National Geographic	*27*
The Past	*28*
There Are Women	*29*
Ancestors	*30*
Coming About	*31*
Rug from the Atlas Mountains	*32*
Arrowheads	*33*
To my Mother and Father	*34*
Tracks	*35*

Zagharit

The Mat	*40*
Petit Pain	*42*
El Biar	*43*
What We Know	*44*

Lullaby   45
Nightlight   46
Maktoub   48
Stone Pines   49
Streetlife   50
Ramy   51
Algiers   52
Water   53
Door   54
Silver Polishing   55
French Doors   56
What Is Written   57
The Days   58
Sabbat   59
Mid–Winter   60
Haircut   61
Courtyard   62
Mint Tea   63
Coastal Route   64
Names of the Disappeared   65
Confluence   66
El Attaf, 1958   67
Zagharit   68

COASTAL

COASTAL

I love your old age,
days when you repeat stories
and the screen door opens
into the parlour of your kitchen.
Your neighbours are without
salt or sugar, wanting to come in
in their tucked-in dresses,

their mops put by,
those tribal processions –
baldness of husbands, sons,
bearded mothers. Fish scaled
and left in the smokehouse,
the sea losing its haze.

They leave behind conversations,
silences, old rope for new.
Your stories tether back
to those first porches.
Who can sleep in the summer months
under such patchwork –
the heat of the past,
the lighthouse room?

The seals have grown old
here too, in the worn-out
quilts of the sea, gusts.
We breathe the same air.
Some nights they look in at us
from the galleries of their whiskers,
streaked with salt, with mating.

I know each moment –
stories that wash up,
coasts that take and take the light,
the first beaten-back mornings.

DEMENTIA

My mother crosses my path.
The winter birches hide and don't hide her
and there is a sense at moments
of a visual lapse, a complicity

as she falls back inevitably
and forgets to finish her sentences,
her scattered thinking. When we talk
there is a forest in her imagination
and one in mine. If we combine them,
the sparse trees she remembers

and those I imagine make up a dense wood
where both of us are reassured and sheltered.
Beyond that we have an understanding.
I know how to calm her – how to turn
these inconsistencies around, fill in the spaces
abandoned now by her memory,
so the day shines and she is still in it.

CAPE PORPOISE, MAINE

I go back to that walk,
island to island
across the mind at low tide –

the sun that dips down
or the flaring sun, dismissing the houses
on the cape, that dimension of the jutting houses

and the way the wind shows them
and then deepens suddenly and is all around me
like a person I know well

and the occasional broken shells
like my mother's unfinished sentences,
her childhood memories I still enjoy visiting.

I go back so I can walk
past my own past into hers
though the tide will come in soon –

as no solution, and with no ambition
but to roll up my bluejeans
and walk where the water was.

STROKE

Sometimes you still say it to me –
sweetdreams, and the glass houses
of New York City rear up,
my comic books piled high in the closet,
what-ifs again, the white radio
I sleep with my arms round,
my window with 81st Street in it.

You're in bed now downstairs,
the walker there beside you.
You're in the red tartan nightgown
I gave you – the window captures you in it –
so thin, winter-thin.
How many forgotten moments are there
in our conversation? The catch in your throat.

I go in search of what is missing,
the mussel-gatherer in the early part of the bay,
wading out. He is there when the sea rises
and the mussels darken and resist
each wave, and when the sea ebbs they shine
and abound and their mouths are tight shut.

OVERLAYS

1

In the snowstorm last certainties appear:
a clinging sunrise, fir trees, spruce and birch
matted close together; occasional windowlight –
smaller and smaller, more personal now –

and then even those are lost, or only restored
briefly. Here where your imagination
could hold out for days, weeks,
not wait to be rescued, to belong anywhere.

2

Deliberately, I make a room of panelled wood
for myself, wood corridors, rooms that reach
into forest nearly, and in this dark
(noon blazing in the crack of the door)

begin confidently to cut and arrange
as you did. I lay out on a table
the lilies and ferns, Indian paintbrushes,
streaks of iris like petrified light.

In that mother-space, grandmother-space
I take up those gestures you had.

3

My child lifts a yellow horse with red wheels
with a great effort and plunges his hand
into its orange rope-mane. He considers
what to do next, how to break up and join
the wooden train that needs so much attention.

A steam train passes through the pine trees
and loosens the pensive, suffocating air.
'Train, train!' we call.
I sit on the hill with my cousins,
clasping my knees.

4

The barn at the top of the hill
holds the shade so steady.
The afternoon is split open,
its spirit divided.

My boy spits out pieces of apple
but keeps them in his soft hand
for another time,
opening and closing his hands,
or because they feel nice,

not cold anymore.
He has four teeth now
an apple can slip through,
the dark brown pips.

5

Soon I will not remember
when it was not always like this.

I climb into a boat on the pond
and immediately a blue heron flies down
into the reeds. There is an effort in its descent
and I am pleased to be alone with it.

On the steep hill above the pond a harvester
is gathering hay. A prolonged silence,
a working silence.

My boat is bent flat, gathered as if to fit into a bottle,
and the harvester is loading the high fields
with tiny bales of hay.

6

I find your drawings of seals riding the waves.
They barely touch the waves, almost clear of them.
And the seals are see-through, like an anguish.

My boy follows a wavy line with his fingers.
At low tide we can still walk out to the islands.
We can walk as far as we can see,
as far as you can remember.

7

The wind is a paper mask I wear.

I can take so little away from here.
On the other hand, the very barrenness
of this island is beautiful.

Our wooden floor tilts.
My boy learns a delicate chain
of actions and reactions.

His bare feet, his soft feet
reach out to the jarring crossing,
dangerous and promising,

that will take him where he wants to be.
Sun, sun, sun – like a stone skipping.

8

My friend Mimi knows where to find blackberries
along the canal to Hackney Marshes.

She shows my boy how to choose the ripe ones
and the red and blue canal boat

makes a lasting reflection in the water
so if you squint it seems to be a house,

nothing less, a house painted by a child,
one I lived in once. It's a kindness –

these blackberries on the hearth of London,
the soot falling among them,

what we rescue wherever we are
and recognise, and take as ours.

FISH-HOUSES

I think of my mother sitting by the waterside,
half in sea. She was never a great swimmer.
She did the breast stroke patiently
and was out of the water quickly.
After her cancer and leg amputation
she couldn't swim, she would roll over and over.
But she liked to be there, right by the edge
as the waves came in, her bathing-skirt billowing,

and she could look for shells and stones,
make the best of just where she was.
For years, her dementia was a long goodbye,
the longest. As when I trudge home
in my sou'wester with my fish, past the fish-houses,
and the light is gone or behind doors only,
the way we are eased into ending
or lie across it, neither in nor out.

COAT

When it was bitter in New York City,
I would go out with my mother
past the icy buildings,

stay against her, just behind her
so she would stop the wind and snow,
and bury my face in her coat,

just there under her arm.
All winter, like her walk-in closet,
its yellow light, I would walk into her,

shake out my raw thoughts.
I didn't know who or what we were passing
or even if the city was still there,

the long radiant hairs against my face
like my grandmother's stole
with a fox's head that lay on her breast,

me clinging to my mortal mother,
our slow progress down that black, warm street.

HAIRPINS

The downpour comes to our house.
All our rooms are ablaze with that inevitable
inconsolable darkness before it ceases

in every room of the house, every part of the woods,
the screened-in porch and white-wood corridor
leading to the window and the whippoorwill

that will turn itself to dust with its song
night after night, cooped up in the willow;
fences and barns and ponds that recede in the rain

but are really constants in my life, come in close,
the pewter magnifying glass on the dresser
magnifying each hour.

My grandmother piles her hair loosely with hairpins.
The hairpins won't hold, never, in that heavy grey.
I push them back for her, her forgetfulness,

and the long summer is almost over
in those few lazy drops that still
drip from the trees and eaves in a lasting vigil.

WHIPPOORWILL

There was always that moment –
the willow slung right against my window
over barns nobody can see,

night in the room when I had chickenpox
and was left to sleep or read or listen only.
The others played dominoes or canasta
or charades downstairs after supper.

What did the whippoorwill look like?
It slept all day for too much light.
My cousin said it was ugly, ragged,
was mottled, speckled.

And it had whiskers by its beak.
It ate moths. My God, I said.
The willow tree stirred, preparing.
I closed my eyes,

afraid to see the whippoorwill
so close to me, as if it were my darling,
its call the one sure thing –
the way dew came right off the grass

in a wave in the morning
when the last cry had disappeared
and I lay in bed shirtless,
dripping with sweat, the scabs tickling.

BLUEBERRY PICKING

I attach my pail to my belt, undo the nets.
Mrs Jessop sits on her porch, wanting talk.
She doesn't drink, just quiet.
A bee buzzes round and round her.
*Take as many as you want. No one
to eat them now Gabriel's gone.*

She has a real moustache like they say
and shaves it. Only the blue stands out
like a stain come through wool.
The sun moves into the porch and away.
Gone a year now she says.
Who'd have thought he'd leave me?

I think of a blue jay, cardinal escaping.
Mrs Jessop's silence, her warding-off smoke.
How I try not to be selfish, try.
The town library with its used-up brink of lawn,
immersion when you enter – books on government,
laws we are learning to obey,

the heron you see over the lake
rarely, late afternoon readers.
Mrs Jessop brings me iced tea and muffins.
I just can't get past it she says softly.

ELVIS

When the record arrived from New York –
over the Panama Canal, down the coast
near Buenaventura, past rotting fruit
you could smell at sea, through Antofagasta,
which is one hot breath for a desert rose,
and into the cool precincts of Santiago

with its stirred cherry trees and magnolias,
they came right over: flat-chested Lorna,
Irene, her freckled bare feet
stained with grass, Rosi
with the muscular legs and long lashes,
Aurora innocent and smiling,

who always arrived late.
We danced to the songs, practising.
We got so good. The song was Anyplace
is Paradise (when I'm with you).
At the time I was reading Wuthering Heights.
That room held me. The mauve-striped shirt

on the record sleeve, the cherry trees
fighting with each other for light
in our garden, for an actual glimpse
over the wall. I would play Anyplace
is Paradise and read Wuthering Heights.
I would play Anyplace is Paradise

and Heathcliff bowed to kiss her
feverishly. Heathcliff in the stable.
Heathcliff weeping. The mauve shirt.
I could see the snow-capped mountains
from my window. The huaso tunes,
the excitement of the nearby huasos

climbing the slopes on their horses,
dead ringers for Heathcliff,
the boys from The Grange, Elvis.
Anyplace. Anyplace is.

In the Paintings of Edward Hopper

May we stop here?
In the filling station
the meter is at zero.

Up and down the laundered
street — it is guesswork
what goes on
behind the open windows.

A face turns from another face
swept into the glare
a small town
dares to withstand.

The eyes could fill with tears.
A wolf could come from the woods
meaning it.

We sap our strength
raking leaves, over coffee,
in a room for the night
or sitting quietly

till daybreak. Houses
take up their old positions
in the wind.

All at once the looseness of fir trees,
the seemliness of our lives.

National Geographic

The bat hands down its X-rayed wings to us,
bones that relay charges of lightning,

and the Sabalites palm in Wyoming
is fossilised in a sediment plate, the fronds
still bravely opening over its stem.

You could fan yourself with it
when the heat waves are visible too,
the palm leaves so exact and excitable

blowing gently inside the rock –
like those soft afternoons on Main Street Anywhere
when everyone has gone away

and it's Sunday or some such closed-up day,
a day without purpose, a magazine day,
impersonal and hot, just you on the street,

the shiny pages flickering:
articulated finger-bones on the X-ray
of a bear's paw, a dolphin's fin,

as if even muscle were irrelevant, extremes of touch.
A naked body painted with clay and water –
all we are,

a man sitting on a sidewalk in his bare feet
kissing his dog, in Fayetteville, West Virginia.

The Past

You can still go there and catch hold –
those silver birches, that river.
You want to have all of it or become it.
You roll your trousers to the knee.

Or you could be far away, decades
could pass and you would still know it
blindfold – steps to the public library,
the mill-bridge, the dry-goods store.

One day you go back to the town
where you have no living connections now –
no longer shoulder to shoulder with it
and the place struggling with you to change

and grow: those dark grey clapboard
houses down the slope and the used cars –
automobile parts dizzied and rusty
in the near-snowstorm, curiosities.

But yes you want to get there anyway,
to those homely things you remember:
a wreath on a door and the yellow light
a house brandishes over the snow

at night that still reaches you somehow
far in the woods where you are breathing
lightly because the cold is crushing you.

There Are Women

Women who let their hair go uncombed,
long, grey, who hold their hair
in their red hands, move in confusion.

Who could cook, or embroider.
Who border the shiver of a man all winter
with their spirit, breathing in the fog air.

Whose clothes are unkempt to this day.
And who move sideways inside their shoes.
Seem meant for love anyways.

Who stand still when the tide overcomes
their large bare feet. Who muddle their sex,
their struggle. Who come in close to him,

whose faces are so close there is nowhere to hide.
Women for whom I would take the combs
from my hair and weep openly, face to face.

ANCESTORS

When I lean down to stir the bathwater
are they reaching down into the river
contours – do they know where I am?

When I am silent do they give up
their own silences like hasty barricades?
Do they root in the shine of river,

grow thoughtful, shine and renew with me
in childhood, adolescence, middle age –
come to each region of my life with me?

Are theirs the gestures I make – forgetful,
candid, slow? And do their sighs
and open-hearted laughs reach out

into the breeze-ways of every small town
I have ever driven through?

COMING ABOUT

As we sail in, land is visible just there
where the fog ends – a holing-out,
a wide entry we carry with us.

We are so ready, our heads lowered
so the boom can pass over us fast
in the shambles of moving across, scurrying
across the deck, the two of us willing to do it,

to hear the slam of the sheet,
turn back as the fog covers all that sea.
We head for the old bookshop on the coast
with its salty reminders, then those rocks,

away from the pier. The reeds push up in the fog,
they are visible and invisible,
they try to take the wind like us, a waiting game.
We come about, the shattering overhead,

the goal imminent as love, and as hard, as surfacy.
We catch onto the first breeze, our open window
over the yawl and low tide, that will take us
into bracing weather and set us down
among people and custom.

Rug from the Atlas Mountains

for Redha

On our knees we examine the weaving:
the folded-in birds, turtles with wayward steps,

horse-figures and butterflies wide as farms,
girls holding hands in a row faded here and there,
camel-shadows – burdened, a grey teapot.

A tree of banners. My mother gave this to us years ago.
The long and tangled threads of wool
under the rug are dark blue and plenty,

white and yellow, brilliant red, bound together
and sticking out like plums, knotted for the duration.
Sometimes we turn the rug over, and it is all still there

just as it always was, still perfectly made –
we are reminded of those intenser hidden colours
that bind, the intricate warmth,

sun fading the surface forms –
how little it takes for you to move me.

ARROWHEADS

There it is, the mark from pencil lead
still embedded in my knee –
all those years of childlessness

like the sooty windows I looked out of
over 57th Street, that took that roar,
not so very far from it all, in earshot.

Or is it somewhere darker, a forest
maybe, where I am searching for flint,
clues, evidence that they were once here

and gone? The Christmas windows
cheerful right up to the fourteenth floor.
The earth is damp, there are ferns,

boulders you could cut an image in.
I am seven again. The smoothed indentations,
nicks, the earth depressed a little

where the arrowheads lay.
A people, peopling these woods.
And they are everywhere.

TO MY MOTHER AND FATHER

I miss you as if you were fiction
and the ink still wet
where we crossed paths –

as if I invented you backwards
with the steam train, the tight grass, downpour,
old solutions I hold to my heart

as my boy holds his coat to his chest
before he puts it on.
I am still trying to understand you.

You become inextricable from Manhattan,
New Hampshire, Martha's Vineyard,
the last reflective windows, uptown din,

the Henry Hudson Parkway,
how many sad entries to the city.
I miss you as if nothing were lost

but only articulated.
And I dream about you.
I pull myself up by my roots.

TRACKS

I

Where there was mire or grass
snow drops from my soles
in thick summery cakes.

Here are the dry bear prints –
just gleams wearing thin.
There is too little of me,

too little pressure, too much of them,
and nothing sticks to me for long.
Here are the tracks of foxes,

wild turkey hurrying past
from dark to dark.
I do not know when you are coming
or who you are.

2

My broom turns up earth and glass,
threads. Snow drips from my roof,
maybe this spring will be real.

The birch trees in the woods pause,
bound together for moments at a time,
then they rock and scrape the clouds
with their totemic heavings.

They throw down branches
and wet bark that once clung to them.
There is so much to achieve in the wind –
a few elderly clouds and then grievous blue
happening where before there was no room for blue,
a cardinal, a chickadee.

On the porch the fleeting spring air
presses through the screen,
all bark shinnying up.

3

The birches unload,
letter-presses, paper mills.

It will be days before I can finish
this cautious unpeeling,
before the stillness is thoroughly worked.

They retrieve and cast away, make light of,
but it is their heaviness I want,
the peeled bark hardly dry

or just imperfectly damp in the spring sun.

4

I was on my way home,
a home-again feeling
running through everywhere –

glimpses of leftover snow, pathways
and where I couldn't go safely
at this hour, pages of a book left open –

then the last wisps of night settling,
houses far away still
but with no darkness in them anymore.

When the deer ran across
just past me, past and past,
I almost felt rather than saw them –

their warmth and how they took up
the whole of that space just ahead of me,
the space that is always there

like an intuition or fear and that finally
turns out to be the most fertile, mud-spattering,
interrupting the terms of my life.

ZAGHARIT

for Ramy

THE MAT

When you first arrived
we put you on a mat
with whatever we had to hand,
a pillowcase, a shawl.
It was June, the shutters were closed
to leave out the dazzling heat of Algiers
so you could rest. I lay down beside you.

You were two and a half months old.
Days before it had been Mouloud
and the fireworks lasted all night.
I had imagined you in your cot
in the children's home hearing the explosions.
Then there were those roars
in the demonstration, tear-gas grenades,
a depot burning and smoke
that billowed over the whole city.

And there were the babies
in the other cots who cried every day,
each in his own abandonment.
For weeks after you came to me
you would sleep with your hands
over your ears.
I wanted to offer you
a kind of quiet here
but I was exhausted already –
just your delicacy and fast
tiny breaths exhausted me,
just the pressure of knowing
you were with me at last.

But I lay down beside you,
I put my face near yours
so I could hear each breath.
Together we began our search for quiet.

Petit Pain

Early mornings I go out to buy the petit pain –
light pastry bread with melted chocolate.
I walk under the apartments with their washing
already hanging from the windows, dripping,
and then down interminable steps,

the remains of rubbish not collected
the night before, past children playing
or leaning on the railings and the locked
cyber-café, to the baker's on the corner
with its double doors wide open,

a few loaves on the glass counter.
I talk a little with the baker and his daughter.
It is plain the confidence they enjoy.
She loads the petits pains and baguettes
into my cloth bag. These are open spaces I cross,

routine now, a festive dust that meets me,
air that is almost tentative,
as if I were listening for you
across a row of manageable distances
while I wait, before we bring you home.

El Biar

The gates open, the intense gates,
the certainty that everything can change
in a moment, stoop like these palm trees,

and that nowhere is more recalcitrant
or remote than what we might find,
who might receive us, where we will sit,

who we will sit among and how they will greet us
warmly or guardedly and look to see you in us,
how we will know you

in your blanket, when they bring you to us.

WHAT WE KNOW

We know where you were born –
in the Parnet hospital at Hussein-Dey.
We know its courtyard of palm
and orange trees, the persistent dust,
we know the low white buildings
and the intricate passages to wards.
We know you were born at 9 pm
when the drought of traffic
still circled around the hospital.
We know that in the morning
the courtyard turned green and yellow
again. My boy, my child –
this much we know.

LULLABY

Even now, I sing the same lullabies
to my baby, the ones I learned
from my father that came down
through Spanish time, cradlewood-time.

My boy caresses my face
with his soft hand, slowly
his hand passes across my face
in that instinctive way
babies have, almost not touching,
almost not caressing.

When I test the heat of the milk
on the inside of my wrist,
it makes a row of tiny drops
and I think of the monks in Poblet
who are sprinkled with holy water
at vespers. How soft and unhurried
I must be for him.

This little boy has no cradle.
His father is a carpenter —
he will make him one
and I stop in the cradle-darkness
and listen to his breathing
in this deep country we live in together.

Nightlight

1

I want to speak about those women
who give birth in secret
but there is a soft hand over my mouth.

I want to ask about those babies
who stay on the ward.
They are there tonight

and tomorrow night.
How is it that they come to be there,
so many of them, oh so many?

2

A few risked palm trees
liberate the walkways,
dry-weeping in the hospital gardens.

They translate word for word
distress, exhaustion of spirit,
into a cursory language –

rushing, distant and cool.

3

The nightlight sets out to find you
over constant waters.
Asking beam partially inked out,
my hand reaching for you.

I was moving south-east, you north-west
along a continuum. But it's as if we were
always in the same room where neither
of us will ever be alone again.

4

At dawn a pencil line, very faint,
red or orange, one drawn fast by a child,
goes back and forth along the sky

with lots of white spaces left.
Secrets I will never know,
that are not mine,

I become used to, and accept
and fold into me, with you.

MAKTOUB

All the interventions of those years,
the interviews and forms, paperwork,

air tickets; and the intentions –
even down to small actions on the day
we met – to drink our coffee, buy croissants,

to get there somehow through the traffic,
find the high wall and stone pines,
to give our names to the security guard,

be brave and decisive, though my hand
trembled. But afterwards the moment
when they brought you to us

would come to seem inevitable –
everything about you that had coincided
with our lives, was already

with us, within us, all that time.

STONE PINES

After you came home I spent days
realising what was gone,
because it was you now and you were real,
you were with us and we had taken on also
what you could never be, or have again.

Soon your passport would be ready.
I thought of the tall and clement
stone pines around the children's home,
softening our leaving through the gates,
as if the goodbye those trees said –

with their fierce guardianship,
their heads so weighed down
delivering up their utmost strength
in retreating, driven inwards, back again
towards the organised interior of the home –

were absolute; so the pressure of waiting
and sleeping lightly was over,
as if a depth had shifted
from there to here.

STREETLIFE

Today is a water day.
I lean out to hang the family washing
under our apartment window.

It's an activity I love, bringing me
in contact with the street –
draping the long sheets first
from the outer lines
where they will receive the best of sun,

then towels and shirts.
I can look down at the women in hijabs
who pass below with their children,
the steaming sheets already giving off
their drenched rustling over the high city

which plummets with them
as far as the port, the sticky breath of sea.
It feels dangerous to be leaning out so far,
the first toiling passers-by never looking up
twice, a politeness, an acknowledgement

that there is nothing strange about my being here,
nothing remarkable about my slow journey
across the long open window.

RAMY

I want to know who cared for him
every day on the ward, whose face
came close to his on the day shift,
the night shift, who held him
and washed him in the original
motions of love, and the doctor
who named him Abdelaziz Ramy.
Ramy – he who aims high,
the archer, who pierces the transparent
cloud over the mountain,
the most arid mountain that ever was –
the one who survives, the survivor.

ALGIERS

I search in the bookshops
for books I will never find
as if its expectations could ever be mine,

its cumulative sadnesses
and rejoicings. Still, it is mine now,
in a way, mine through you –

this bursting city, where the connections
to me loosen and give way
and then bind me round and round

in hope for it – in hope for its streets
and steps of children who push past me
in their eagerness for the moment

and call out to each other – Mehdi, Karim,
Omar, Abdellatif, Ramy.

WATER

Today they have washed out the huge
plastic storage jars ready for the water
with a little bleach and when the water arrives
we will scrub the tiled floors in our bare feet,
we will stand in water, and fill all the empty
mineral-water and coca-cola bottles
and the bathtub. I will wash out your
tiny vests and hang them from the line
on the veranda, one peg each
where they will dry immediately.
On the latticework veranda the blue
plastic bowl will shiver with water,
water will know where dust is,
what dust is news, and take over.
Later Sihem will pour water over my hair
so it splashes on the veranda everywhere,
everywhere but I will hardly see it
for night, and I will celebrate and work
and remember the dry days without you.

Door

A woman lives here.
I can barely squeeze past
the almost-closed entrance
to her apartment building,

the tangled evening beyond,
residents' post-boxes
with absolutely nothing in them,
no destinations, the stairwell

where I become dizzy climbing
and have to sit down for a long time
while her relatives brush past me
and greet me gently.

There is no give in it,
sleep-holding, sleep-housing.
But a child can get in easily.
That you cannot close.
That I cannot close.

SILVER POLISHING

Now I know what this quiet labour is.
My hands hurt. A candlelight,
a way of lifting the haze from things,

fingers round a tiny wrist,
circle within circle,
the pressure steadily removing –
my mother's baby cup, 1914,

battered and dimpled, rocking on its base.
As if a last politeness could go all at once
and what is really there appear,
my grandmother's deep silver spoons

laid out on newspaper down the long table –
if only, only
you can see your face in them at last.

French Doors

The French doors are open
and you are striking a toy drum
with red and green stripes.

You are ringing a bell in an orange plastic cage
and shaking yellow maracas.
You drag an articulated ceramic grasshopper

with a hat across the floor.
And then you say *g-rah* with a rolled *r* –
and *bukkhé* and *bukkheki*

because these are the early sounds
of your contentment.
I touch the strings of my guitar

you so softly stroke with your warm hand –
not looking for melody, not yet.

What Is Written

The way you look at your book:
crawl round, lie over it,
turn numbers of pages at a time
and sit and put your face down
to look deeply into the words,

lay your arm across
to turn the pages backwards
and force your whole body round
so you can read the book upside down.
Then you squat and lean on both hands

as if resting forever on the two sides,
the two open pages given to you
at that moment, like something wanting
you can only make sense of
by turning round and round,

your socks working themselves off.
And then you step on the book
in your bare feet, sliding across it.

THE DAYS

The days are going now, the beautiful days.
You run after them.
Even after I have packed away your summer clothes
you drag them out –

Orange shorts, orange shorts
you cry, holding them to you.
I know well what's in store:
jamjars stoppered with wax,

apples, sore throats, bright red throats,
falling leaves that hide us
and that I try to explain to you,
my hem you step on to stop me going.

Sabbat

Now the Algerian words begin too,
arwah for come here, *sabbat* for shoe –
a way of earthing what you know
in your father's culture, like the Spanish
zapato that opens the Madrid streets
of my own father in my mind
so I enter the cobbler's of his time
where everything is black, blackened
for a moment, away from the sun.
Your shoes are lined up on the stairs,
your dark green wellies and the yellow
slippers you never want to wear
and your red and blue leather shoes
with a patch of suede and powerful laces,
size 6. You bring your shoes to your father
holding them against your chest
and put them down on his lap
and then lie down on the floor
with your feet held up a bit,
waiting for him to put them on for you
so you can go out into his world with him.

MID-WINTER

These days fold over us, dark, oppressive,
giving of cold only, so the yellow
burrows into windows and language
becomes clarified and sharp, everlasting,
as if the cold were a whetting-stone for words.

All winter long the premonition of words.
You come between me and language,
your warm face between me and my book,
pulling yourself up on the bed
as you pull yourself up on your first words:
gee, give me, or *atini* in Algerian.

And I imagine you talking fluently,
as if you could rise now from these layers
of wool and quilt and walk out
confidently into the ice and wind
and a world impatient for you.

HAIRCUT

A woman is cutting your hair.
You are among us in the shadows,
the fast warm shadows in a patio,
and you are sitting on my lap.
There is a swift sequence of events,
the scissors easily snip the curls
here and there and the day evens out
behind the mulberry trees
with their cool, fat leaves succulent
for the goats. The mountains are rarely seen,
mostly hidden by the trees,
and the goats in the mud yard below
will eat the mulberry leaves
and then the tree will make more.
Come quickly mountains, goats, hens –
come and see my son, shorn, calm,
the women in attendance,
among the staunch mulberry leaves.

COURTYARD

A fresh start each time
she splashes water over the courtyard
and then pushes, sweeps it across –

her hair newly hennaed, wrapped
in a scarf, this over-clean courtyard
that constantly refreshes us,

water that evaporates fast
and is replenished fast
so her guests feel comfortable and cool.

Here all those years ago, before you,
I felt the sadness of my childlessness,
her small children running in and out,

the pear tree extending over the wall
like an eager neighbour,
but found some relief in the steady

rush of water, the inevitable joyous splash
from the bucket, and sweeping it up
and away, feeling helpful and included.

MINT TEA

The glass tumblers are tiny,
gold-rimmed or embossed
or filigreed with green or crimson

so the taste is seen, sipped,
not urged on us, nothing urgent,
just the divination of taste

among laughter and talk.
We sit in the open courtyard
in your grandmother's village

and you run off to play
with Ikram and Sabiha
and Jawida. You all lie down

on your backs in a circle,
your feet pointing to the centre,
and make a star, down here on earth.

COASTAL ROUTE

We had been to the hospital
where you were born, just to see it.
We sat on the grass in the courtyard
under the palm trees, and then your uncle
drove us back to Zeralda along the old,
slow coastal road west out of Algiers,
because the fast highway was clogged.

We drove through Bab El Oued,
La Pointe Pescade, Bélvèdere, Bainem,
the tracking of feeling, shop fronts,
hardware, the coast where your father
used to swim as a boy, rocks, high rocks
so many boys still jump from,
and low painted houses

right out to the softer country.
We were looking for something that day –
what was it? A beachball, sandals for you?
Or was it mint wrapped in newspaper
you could hide your face in?
What had I gone over in my mind?
How many doors opened along the way?

NAMES OF THE DISAPPEARED

We go out into the sunlight of Algiers.
There is a pool of sun on each street.
Each street has tall houses, balconies,
mouldings and awnings, tracery.

We take hold of the street with our hands
to deliver it – there are crowds now,
flower vendors, vendors of canaries and parakeets
and parrots, of doves in small cages
or black plastic plates with cloth roses,

daisies and gold inscriptions: *Félicitations*
pour le bébé et prompt rétablissement
à la maman, vendors of key rings
with names painted on varnished wood:
Mourad, Djamel, Aicha, Mohamed,

Ali, Mouloud, Hassan, Amar.
The street is intricate, holds us,
it is in the imperative. We return
to the turquoise parakeet, the green parakeet
with plush black markings,

to the dove in the tight cage with its eyes closed
and those hundreds of names on key rings.
In the Rue Didouche Mourad the trees
join in a difficult embrace
and there we walk in peace and shade
as if we will never be parted.

Confluence

At moments, when you laugh or embrace me
there is a shadow-you in my mind, delving inside
the true places I lived once –

or who you are joins with a you
growing up with me, never to be realised,
sharing my mother's embrace, her laugh

and this confluence is the fresh start a river constantly
makes when it joins another –
a new river-shadow in the old river

till the two are indistinguishable –
that's how close you come to who I was
cast lengthways and unbroken in me.

EL ATTAF, 1958

There are also tracts I am not sure of,
stones pulled away from the earth,
days when the wheat was ready,

preparations in farmhouses for war —
and all the time the simple, sincere light
across the plain that stops short,

a soldier praying in an open field,
your father a child no older than you,
sitting on a wall, legs swinging.

Soon his own father would be gone
and the war would take his uncles
and brother. Forgiveness and fear.

Forgive me for not knowing those days.
Your father brings them to you
when he says your name and leans down
to kiss you. You are from his country.

ZAGHARIT

I ask them how they do it —
how they make it —
the *youyou* cry, *zagharit,*
memorable and elemental,
that could carry ships, lift a child,
celebrate a revolution.

The women are here
in beaded dresses and they dance
upstairs in a separate room,
they dress you, three years old
in a white satin shirt
and a crimson waistcoat
with gold embroidery.

You are wearing white satin billowing
trousers and pointed slippers, gold
and crimson just like the waistcoat,
and a crimson and gold cap over your curls.
Your father, his cousins, our friends
are waiting downstairs
and you keep taking off the cap
and we keep putting it back on.

And when everything is ready —
the lace frill on your shirt —
we all stand at the top of the stairs
and the women begin to cry
that piercing, throbbing continuous cry
that is the transformation of pain,
or the creation of pain
to make room for joy,

and I take you by the hand
and the women follow you downstairs
into the bright company.